W9-BNR-833

Fetch

HOW A BAD DOG BROUGHT ME HOME

ALSO BY NICOLE J. GEORGES

Invincible Summer

Calling Dr. Laura

The names and faces of some humans in this book have been changed.

Copyright © 2017 by Nicole J. Georges

ALL RIGHTS RESERVED

For information about permission to reproduce selections from this book,

write to trade.permissions@hmhco.com or to Permissions,

Houghton Mifflin Harcourt Publishing Company, 3 Park Avenue, 19th Floor,

New York, New York 10016.

www.hmhco.com

Library of Congress Cataloging-in-Publication Data is available

ISBN 978-0-544-57783-1

Printed in China

SCP 10 9 8 7 6 5 4 3 2 1

Lyrics from "Freewheel" by the band Team Dresch © 1995, used with permission.

Production assistance by Asher Craw.

for my dog

TABLE of CONTENTS

BEIJA'S PARTY HAD STREAMERS AND BALLOONS, DOG TOYS AND TREATS, A VEGAN GRILL AND MY FRIENDS. ALL TO CELEBRATE THE LONG LIFE AND HEALTH OF MY FIERCE AND SENSITIVE BEST FRIEND.

THE THING WAS, EVERYONE KNEW MY DOG HATED KIDS. SHE BARELY TOLERATED ADULTS, AND MADE NO MYSTERY OF HER FEELINGS ABOUT CHILDREN THROUGH LUNGING, GROWLING, AND A REPUTATION FOR FREQUENT LEAPING.

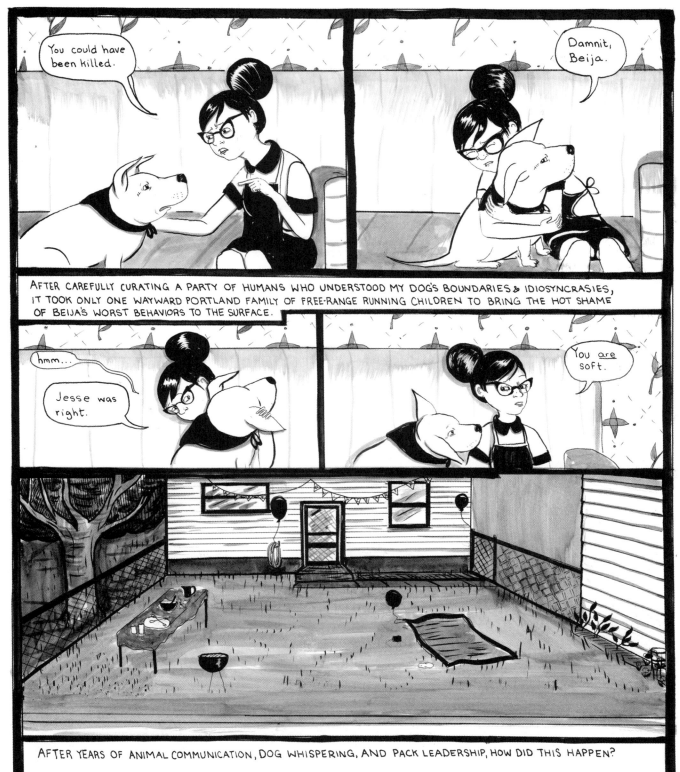

I COULD HAVE PUT BEIJA IN HER KENNEL, TUNED OUT THE BARKING, AND CHOSEN TO GO UPSTAIRS WITHOUT HER. I COULD EVEN HAVE GIVEN THIS DOG UP AT THE FIRST SIGN OF HER BEHAVIOR ISSUES, HER "BADNESS."

BUT I WOULD NEVER DO ANY OF THOSE THINGS. AS IT WAS, I HAD OWNED AND LOVED THIS DECIDEDLY BAD DOG FROM MY CHILDHOOD TO ADULTHOOD, AND SHE WAS AS MUCH A PART OF ME AS I WAS OF HER.

1. Come

I GOT THE JOB FOR THE HOLIDAY SEASON, IN ORDER TO PAY FOR MY BOYFRIEND'S BIG CHRISTMAS PRESENT.

I NEEDED $40 TO ADOPT A DOG FROM THE POUND, AND I WORKED TOWARD THIS GOAL BY THE HOUR, $3.75 AT A TIME.

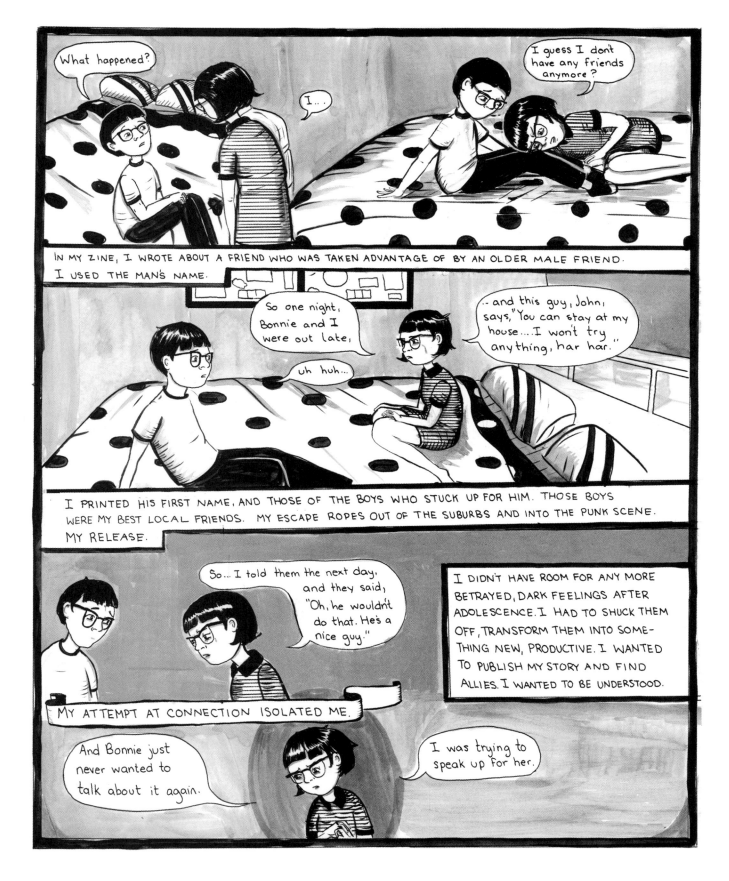

What happened?

I...

I guess I don't have any friends anymore?

IN MY ZINE, I WROTE ABOUT A FRIEND WHO WAS TAKEN ADVANTAGE OF BY AN OLDER MALE FRIEND. I USED THE MAN'S NAME.

So one night, Bonnie and I were out late,

uh huh...

..and this guy, John, says, "You can stay at my house....I won't try anything, har har."

I PRINTED HIS FIRST NAME, AND THOSE OF THE BOYS WHO STUCK UP FOR HIM. THOSE BOYS WERE MY BEST LOCAL FRIENDS. MY ESCAPE ROPES OUT OF THE SUBURBS AND INTO THE PUNK SCENE. MY RELEASE.

So... I told them the next day, and they said, "Oh, he wouldn't do that. He's a nice guy."

I DIDN'T HAVE ROOM FOR ANY MORE BETRAYED, DARK FEELINGS AFTER ADOLESCENCE. I HAD TO SHUCK THEM OFF, TRANSFORM THEM INTO SOMETHING NEW, PRODUCTIVE. I WANTED TO PUBLISH MY STORY AND FIND ALLIES. I WANTED TO BE UNDERSTOOD.

MY ATTEMPT AT CONNECTION ISOLATED ME.

And Bonnie just never wanted to talk about it again.

I was trying to speak up for her.

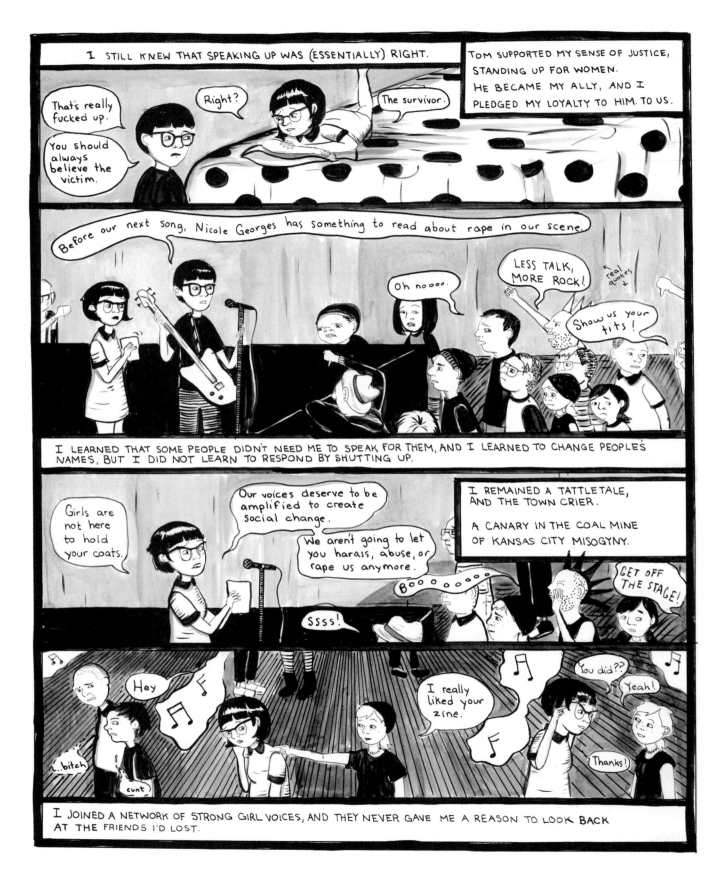

THE AIR WAS THICK WITH BARKING AND A GAMEY SMELL THAT I WAS ACTIVELY DENYING.

EVERY DOG MANUAL WILL TELL YOU NOT TO PICK THE DOG HIDING IN THE BACK OF THE CAGE.

A SHY DOG IS MORE LIKELY TO BITE AND WILL OFTEN BECOME A FEARFUL, ANTISOCIAL ADULT.

Hi, Roxy

How are you?

thump

thump

thump

!!!

Let's take this one outside!

WHAT THEY DO NOT TELL YOU IS THAT THIS DOG WILL SWEETLY STARE AT YOU THROUGH THE BARS OF HER CAGE, AND START BEATING HER TAIL AGAINST THE METAL FLOOR OF HER ENCLOSURE AT THE SOUND OF YOUR VOICE.

THERE IS NOTHING IN ANY MANUAL INSTRUCTING HOW TO DEFEND YOURSELF AGAINST A DOG WITH INFLATABLE EARS.

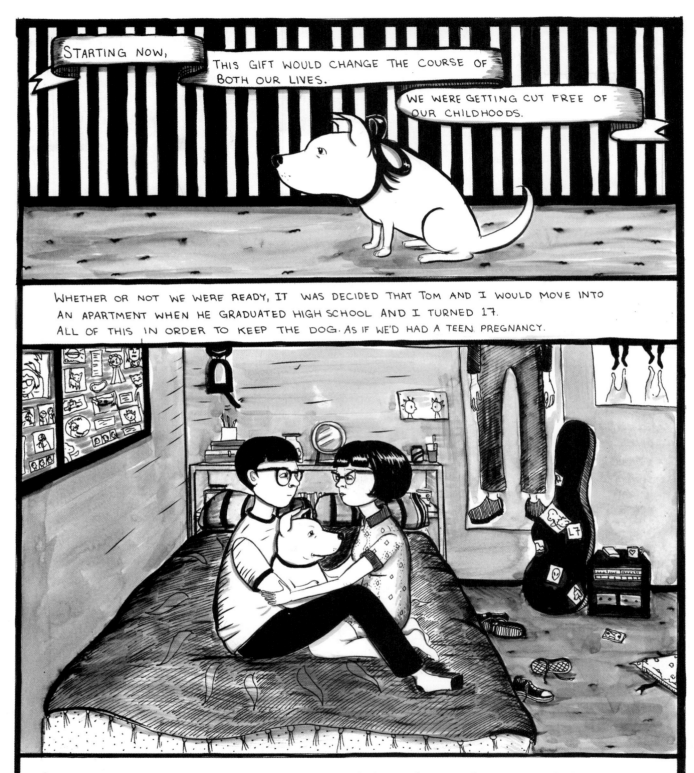

STARTING NOW, THIS GIFT WOULD CHANGE THE COURSE OF BOTH OUR LIVES.

WE WERE GETTING CUT FREE OF OUR CHILDHOODS.

WHETHER OR NOT WE WERE READY, IT WAS DECIDED THAT TOM AND I WOULD MOVE INTO AN APARTMENT WHEN HE GRADUATED HIGH SCHOOL AND I TURNED 17. ALL OF THIS IN ORDER TO KEEP THE DOG. AS IF WE'D HAD A TEEN PREGNANCY.

IN THE MEANTIME, SHE WOULD REMAIN A GUEST IN MY PARENTS' HOME. DESPITE THEIR RELIGIOUS BELIEFS ABOUT COHABITATION BEFORE MARRIAGE, MY PARENTS' DESIRE FOR A BEIJA-FREE HOME WAS STRONGER.

BEIJA BECAME EVEN LESS POPULAR IN OUR FAMILY ONCE SHE BEGAN PEEING ON THE CARPET AND EATING THE FURNITURE. IF PACO EVER FOLLOWED SUIT, IT WAS ALWAYS ASSUMED THAT BEIJA CORRUPTED HIM.

SHE COULD LEAP EXTRAORDINARILY WELL FOR SOMEONE WITH FOUR-INCH LEGS. SHE REGULARLY BALANCED ON THE SECOND-STORY DECK RAILING.

THE DOG LEAPT DIRECTLY INTO MY MOM'S HERB GARDEN, WHERE SHE GOT BUSTED AFTER BECOMING TOO SCARED TO HOP OUT.

JUST BECAUSE I'D INCREASED MY TEEN RESPONSIBILITIES DIDN'T MEAN MY FRIENDS COULD FOLLOW SUIT.

EVEN AFTER MY DENTAL TRAUMA, I WAS PACIFIED WITH SUGAR. PROBLEMS WERE DEALT WITH IN THE QUICKEST, IF NOT HEALTHIEST, WAYS.

I NEVER FOLLOWED RULES BECAUSE THERE WERE NO RULES, JUST THE QUESTIONABLE EFFICIENCY OF QUICK FIXES.

I ONLY FELT THE EDGES OF OUR WORLD WHEN I ACCIDENTALLY CROSSED THEM.

WITH THE AMOUNT OF STRUCTURE I WAS GIVEN, ONE COULD LOGICALLY COME TO THE CONCLUSION I'D HAVE BEEN BETTER OFF IN A WOLF PACK.

RAISED BY WOLVES, I WOULD HAVE FALLEN IN LINE WITH THE ORGANIZATION AND CONTROL OF MY FELLOW PACKMATES,

WITH A JOB AND BOUNDARIES AND AN IDEA OF HOW TO BEHAVE.

I REGRESSED FROM POTTY TRAINING, COMPULSIVELY RUBBED ON THE CORNER OF THE COUCH,

AND FRACTURED MY ARM JUMPING BED TO BED UNSUPERVISED (A TRICK MY MOM TAUGHT ME).

I HAD A GOOD TIME BEING WILD,

BUT I HAD NO IDEA THESE THINGS WERE NOT NORMAL.

GIVEN MY OWN UPBRINGING, IMAGINE, THEN, THE FATE OF THE MANY PETS UNDER MY CARE.

WHEN PRISSY DISAPPEARED, NEVER TO RETURN, I WAS DEVASTATED. MY FIRST LOSS, AND MY FIRST MEETING WITH DEATH, WAS BARELY EXPLAINED, AND NEVER ADDRESSED BY MY MOM.

MAYBE THE CAT WAS TIRED, OR SICK, BUT ALL I UNDERSTOOD IS WE WERE APART AND I WAS FORLORN.

WHEN MY MOTHER WOULD YELL AT ME, OR TURN SHORT-TEMPERED AND DISMISSIVE, I RAN UPSTAIRS TO MY ROOM AND STARED INTENTLY AT A PHOTOGRAPH OF OUR DEAD CAT.

2. Stay

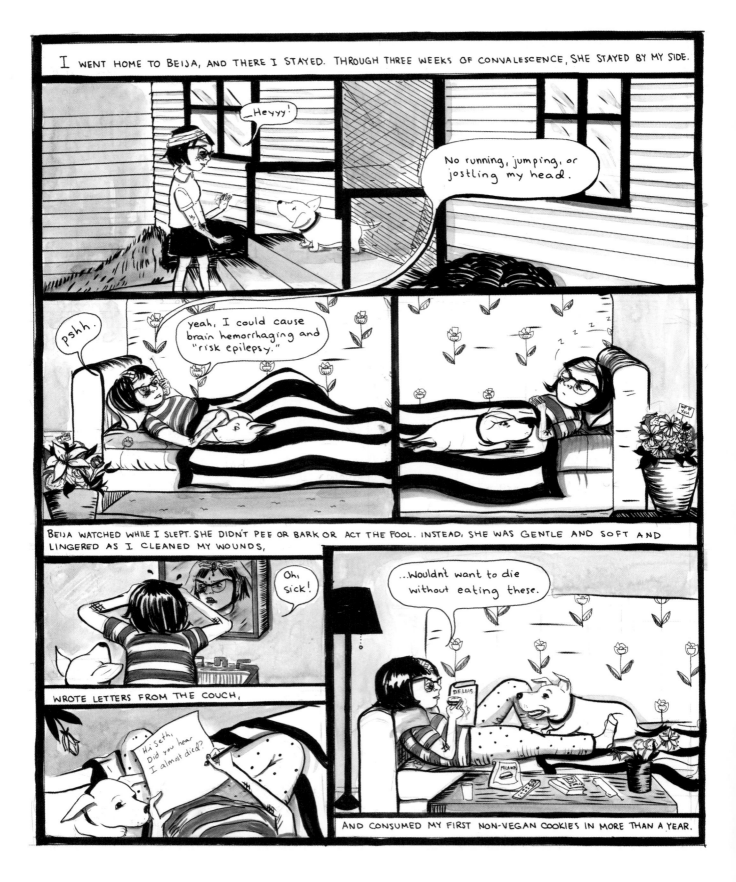

TOM AND I COULDN'T RIDE IN CARS WITHOUT CRYING,   AND WE MISSED OUR COLLEGE APPLICATION DEADLINES.

BUT THERE WAS STILL THE PROBLEM OF THIS BEAST.

SO WITH OUR FUTURES ON HOLD, WE DECIDED TO GET AN APARTMENT.

MY PARENTS' CATHOLICISM TURNED A BLIND EYE TO MY TEEN SCHEME.

TO KEEP US NEAR AND BEIJA FAR, THEY CO-SIGNED ON AN APARTMENT IN MIDTOWN KANSAS CITY, MISSOURI.

THE APARTMENT HAD A NO-PETS POLICY, WHICH SHOULD HAVE BEEN A DEAL-BREAKER, BUT MY DISREGARD FOR RULES, AND THE FACT THAT THEY'D RENT TO TEENAGERS, MADE ME CERTAIN THAT EVERYTHING WOULD WORK OUT OKAY...

WHEN I CAME HOME FROM WORK ON LUNCH BREAK, I WAS MET WITH A HOSTILE LANDLORD.

BEIJA WAS ADOPTED BY A GREEN-HAIRED PUNK GIRL NAMED RUSTY, WHO LIVED IN A DOG-FRIENDLY HOUSE WITH HER DRUMMER BOYFRIEND, DAVE.

THE HAND-OFF WAS SURPRISINGLY EASY. IT FELT LIKE SHE WAS STAYING WITH FAMILY.

RUSTY AND DAVE WALKED BEIJA AROUND THE NEIGHBORHOOD EVERY DAY, AND SAID SHE MADE THEIR LIVES FEEL COMPLETE.

My original designs for Beija had been foiled so long ago, before Christmas even, that I'd let go of my dreams of her healing Tom's heart.

I didn't even realize mine was on the table.

Beija had come into the picture, split up our families, and caused me so much anxiety that now I just wanted her to have a good home, even if it wasn't with me. I wanted a happy outcome for the temperamental beast.

I was relaxing into this idea of Rusty's being her forever home when Beija was abruptly returned.

84

WHEN MY FEET WERE TO THE COALS, I WROTE A LETTER TO MY LANDLORD.

We love our apartment and look forward to living here for a long time. I know our lease says "no pets", but through a set of circumstances, our dog Beija has been returned to us & we cannot find her another home. She is going to stay with us. She is small & house-trained & sweet. If this is a problem, we will have to break our lease. We would really like to stay, and are even willing to pay a pet deposit.
Sincerely, Nicole + Tom

I WAS INSPIRED TO BEND THE STATED RULES BY MY OWN MOTHER, WHOSE IMPASSIONED MISSIVE TO THE HEAD OF ST. THOMAS AQUINAS HIGH SCHOOL KEPT

ME ENROLLED FOR A YEAR, DESPITE THEIR DEMANDS THAT I DYE MY HAIR A "NATURAL COLOR" AFTER ARRIVING ONE DAY WITH HARD-EARNED BLUE-GRAY TRESSES.

If you made every bottle-blonde I see in that parking lot stay home until her hair was its natural color, you wouldn't have a school. Mother Superior, I ask that you allow my daughter the same courtesy.
Sometimes life isn't black and white, sometimes it's shades of gray.
Sincerely, Sabine

MANAGER

OUR LANDLORD NEVER RESPONDED.

So... it's okay?

IN A TWIST OF LUCK, OUR NEW NEIGHBORS WERE A DEAF WOMAN, AND A NURSE WHO WORKED ALMOST EVERY HOUR WE WERE OUT OF THE HOUSE.

ARRP! ARRRP!

THE ABSENCE OF COMPLAINTS GAVE US THE TIME AND SPACE TO TRY TO TRAIN OUR MISBEHAVING DOG.

whine   whine

TOM WORKED ON HER ABANDONMENT ANXIETY BY LEAVING THE HOUSE FOR SHORT INCREMENTS ON HIS DAYS OFF, AND ALWAYS RETURNING WHEN SHE DIDN'T BARK.

Good girl!!!

No, no!

She's shy!

grrrr

DESPITE OUR BEST EFFORTS,

BEIJA WAS VERY MUCH A WORK IN PROGRESS.

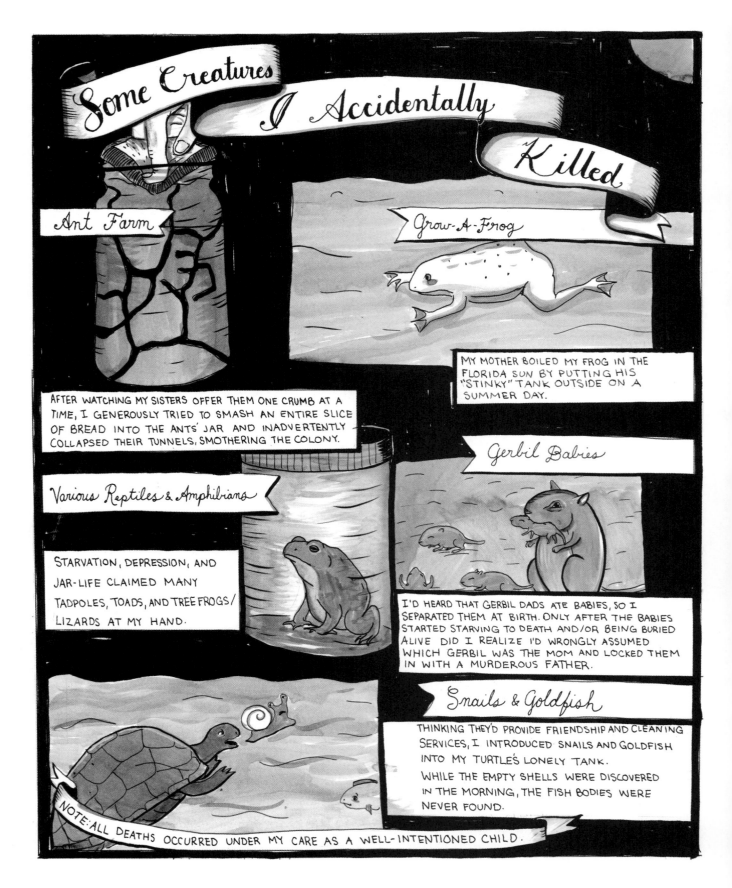

Some Creatures I Accidentally Killed

Ant Farm

Grow-A-Frog

MY MOTHER BOILED MY FROG IN THE FLORIDA SUN BY PUTTING HIS "STINKY" TANK OUTSIDE ON A SUMMER DAY.

AFTER WATCHING MY SISTERS OFFER THEM ONE CRUMB AT A TIME, I GENEROUSLY TRIED TO SMASH AN ENTIRE SLICE OF BREAD INTO THE ANTS' JAR AND INADVERTENTLY COLLAPSED THEIR TUNNELS, SMOTHERING THE COLONY.

Various Reptiles & Amphibians

Gerbil Babies

STARVATION, DEPRESSION, AND JAR-LIFE CLAIMED MANY TADPOLES, TOADS, AND TREE FROGS/ LIZARDS AT MY HAND.

I'D HEARD THAT GERBIL DADS ATE BABIES, SO I SEPARATED THEM AT BIRTH. ONLY AFTER THE BABIES STARTED STARVING TO DEATH AND/OR BEING BURIED ALIVE DID I REALIZE I'D WRONGLY ASSUMED WHICH GERBIL WAS THE MOM AND LOCKED THEM IN WITH A MURDEROUS FATHER.

Snails & Goldfish

THINKING THEY'D PROVIDE FRIENDSHIP AND CLEANING SERVICES, I INTRODUCED SNAILS AND GOLDFISH INTO MY TURTLE'S LONELY TANK.
WHILE THE EMPTY SHELLS WERE DISCOVERED IN THE MORNING, THE FISH BODIES WERE NEVER FOUND.

NOTE: ALL DEATHS OCCURRED UNDER MY CARE AS A WELL-INTENTIONED CHILD.

WE MOVED FROM MARYLAND TO FLORIDA WHEN I WAS SIX, WHEN MY MOM FOLLOWED SOME AWFUL MAN THERE. IN THIS NEW CLIMATE, MY ROOM BECAME THE AMPHIBIAN EQUIVALENT OF A LIVE GAME HUNTER'S TROPHY ROOM.

THE CREATURES LINING MY WALLS WERE DESTINED FOR SHORT LIVES WITHIN PEANUT BUTTER JARS WHOSE LIDS PROVIDED HOME-STABBED AIR HOLES.

MY PET TURTLE, SEAWEED, SWAM NEARBY,

AND A GERBIL FAMILY CHEWED TUBES NERVOUSLY FROM WITHIN AN AQUARIUM, AWAITING THEIR NEXT FORCED PETTING,

I RECEIVED NO TRAINING IN ANIMAL CARE AND MAINTENANCE, ONLY NETS AND MORE JARS IN RESPONSE TO MY UNBRIDLED ENTHUSIASM AND DEVOTION TO CAPTURING THE CREATURES OF OUR NEW NEIGHBORHOOD.

WITH MY LAX UPBRINGING, I ONLY PERIODICALLY ATTENDED ELEMENTARY SCHOOL; AND SO I HAD PLENTY OF TIME TO SPEND WITH MY PETS.

I SPENT MY DAYS GETTING FAT ON RICH CHOCOLATE AND TELEVISION, WRITING IN MY DIARY, AND ORDERING PIZZAS WITH MY MOM'S FOUND CHECKBOOK.

ALL WHILE MY GERBILS MATED AND MY TURTLE KNOCKED AROUND IN HER TANK, SWIMMING LAPS TO NOWHERE.

IT FELT LIKE I HAD A LOT TO DO, AND SCHOOL WAS JUST A NUISANCE. AN OBSTACLE IN THE WAY OF MY IMMEDIATE, DR DOOLITTLE DESIRES.

I HAD NO CONSCIENCE ABOUT MISSING SCHOOL, ONLY THE MOMENTARY ANXIETY OF TRYING NOT TO BE SEEN WHEN I DID RETURN. I DIDN'T WANT ANYONE'S JUDGMENT OR NOTICE TO PENETRATE MY TIME. IF I KEPT UNDER THE RADAR, I HOPED TO GET AWAY WITHOUT DOING ANY SCHOOLWORK AT ALL.

I RAN FREQUENT COLD BATHS FOR MY TURTLE, SEAWEED, AND CONDUCTED EXPERIMENTS TO SEE WHICH SONGS SHE SWAM BEST TO. I WAS CONVINCED SHE WAS INTELLIGENT, AND HATCHED PLANS TO UNLOCK HER TRUE POTENTIAL BY TEACHING SEAWEED TO READ.

95

I WOULDN'T MAKE THE CONNECTION BETWEEN ANIMAL HARM AND MY DINNER PLATE FOR ANOTHER FEW YEARS, BUT IN THE MEANTIME, I BONDED WITH ANIMALS AS MUCH AS I COULD.

ohhh, beautiful!

Over-handling,

Dress-Up

BAT

and Literacy

I WAS GIVING THEM LOVE, BUT I WAS GIVING THEM WHAT I CONSIDERED LOVE. JUST LIKE MY MOTHER TREATING ME TO RODENTS AND CANDY AND ENDLESS SUMMERTIMES, IN LIEU OF DOCTORS AND ELEMENTARY SCHOOL. MY CARE WAS DOLED OUT NARCISSISTICALLY, A DIRTY MIRROR THAT MISSED THE MARK ON PRIMARY NEED AND BASIC COMFORT OR STRUCTURE.

THE VISITING AMPHIBIANS GENERALLY SERVED OUT THEIR JAR TIME ONLY TO DIE IN PRISON, STARVED AND DEPRESSED, UNLESS MY SISTER MEG STEPPED IN BEHIND MY BACK AND SET THEM FREE.

Come on, let's go.

WHERE'S PRINCESS LITTLE FOOT?!??

MEG.

I LEARNED EMPATHY EVENTUALLY,

Look at this, Jordan!

ONCE I HAD MORE MAMMALS ON HAND.

I LEARNED THIS THROUGH A SERIES OF BOOKS.

THE MRS. PIGGLE-WIGGLE SERIES FEATURED A WIZARDLY GRANDMOTHER CHARACTER

WHO USED HER HANDICRAFT MAGIC TO TEACH CHILDREN VALUABLE LESSONS IN LIFE.

DON'T BE A CRYBABY,

BATHING IS NOT OPTIONAL,

owl!

AND SHOW COMPASSION TOWARD YOUR ANIMAL FRIENDS.

In "The Pet Forgetter Cure," a little girl with an ill-tended home menagerie gets sent to Mrs. Piggle-Wiggle's farm.

When young Rebecca Rolfe forgets to feed the animals at the farm, Mrs. Piggle-Wiggle "accidentally" locks her out of the house, where she is left hungry and sad. She is forced to face the punitive anger of her furry & feathered former friends, all a direct result of her irresponsible behavior.

3. Leave It

WE CHOSE TO MOVE TO PORTLAND ON A WHIM.

THE NEED TO LEAVE KANSAS CITY WAS STRONG, BUT THE DESTINATION WAS LESS SET.

WE HAD A VAGUE IDEA THAT THERE WAS A COLLEGE IN PORTLAND CALLED REED, AND THAT WAS ENOUGH TO CONVINCE OUR PARENTS, WHO HAD LOST INTEREST IN THE COLLEGE PUSH ONCE TOM AND I WERE OUT OF THE HOUSE.

Tom, we are going to get you that deposit back!

Thanks, Mom,

but it's not likely after all the dog pee.

Hey look, Beija-Boo is helping clean, too!

I COULD SEE MOUNTAINS FROM MY ROOFTOP AND A DOG PARK ACROSS THE STREET. IT RAINED A LITTLE ALL THE TIME, AND THIS PLACE WAS MINE.

WRESTLING PARTY! 7PM
PIE EATING CONTEST!
Bands!
Fist Fite
Jonny X & the Groadies
and more
642 FREMONT ST

WE FELT LIKE ADULTS, BUT SHOWED OUR AGE BY INAUGURATING OUR FREMONT STREET HOME WITH A WRESTLING PARTY AND PUNK SHOW.

WE POSTED FLIERS ALL OVER OUR NEW TOWN. ON THE NIGHT OF THE SHOW, YOUNG PUNKS CAME OUT IN DROVES.

I LOCKED BEIJA IN MY BEDROOM.

109

watch out!

EVERYTHING WE HAD WAS MAKESHIFT AND IMPERFECT. VINTAGE, BUT CHIPPED. LIKE THE BOXCAR CHILDREN:

OUR TREASURED MID-CENTURY FORMICA TABLE WHOSE METAL LEGS SWAYED WHEN YOU LEANED ON IT,

THE FLUFFY BEIGE CARPET, NOW MOTTLED WITH THICK DOG-PEE STAINS,

AND EVERY 1960s DRESS I OWNED, WHOSE HEM WAS FIXED WITH STAPLES.

MY STAINS WERE DRAWN OVER IN SHARPIE,

AND SHIRTS HELD CLOSED ONLY WITH THE GRACE OF SAFETY PINS.

Perfect.

NOTHING CAME NEW, OR REALLY NICE, BUT WE DIDN'T SEEM TO NOTICE. WE DIDN'T KNOW ANY DIFFERENT. IT DIDN'T SEEM TO MATTER.

OUR COLLEGE AMBITIONS DIDN'T PASS MUSTER WITH OUR NEW FRIENDS.

Maybe we'll go to Reed.

yuck

WE SOON REALIZED IT WAS VERY EXPENSIVE, WE COULDN'T AFFORD TUITION, AND ALL OF THE PUNKS DISLIKED "REEDIES" FOR BEING PRIVILEGED ENOUGH TO LEARN THERE.

I DID ZINES AND MUSIC AND BIKE-RIDING INSTEAD, MAINTAINING MY CRED, BUT ESCHEWING EDUCATION.

momentum makes myyyyy head

I KEPT MINIMUM-WAGE JOBS TO SUPPORT MY ART HABIT.

112

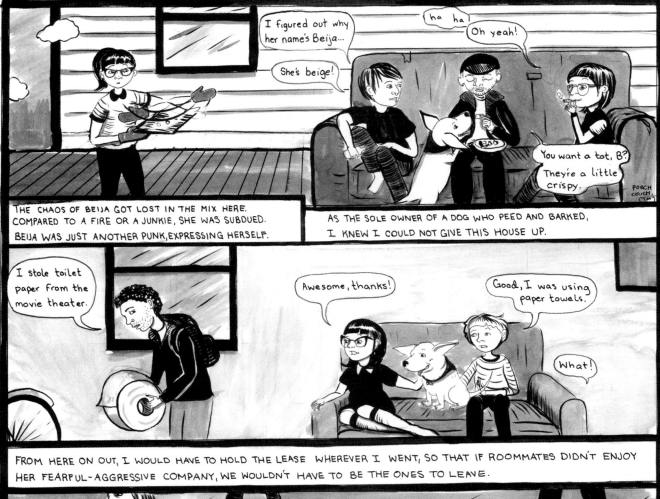

THE CHAOS OF BEIJA GOT LOST IN THE MIX HERE. COMPARED TO A FIRE OR A JUNKIE, SHE WAS SUBDUED. BEIJA WAS JUST ANOTHER PUNK, EXPRESSING HERSELF.

AS THE SOLE OWNER OF A DOG WHO PEED AND BARKED, I KNEW I COULD NOT GIVE THIS HOUSE UP.

FROM HERE ON OUT, I WOULD HAVE TO HOLD THE LEASE WHEREVER I WENT, SO THAT IF ROOMMATES DIDN'T ENJOY HER FEARFUL-AGGRESSIVE COMPANY, WE WOULDN'T HAVE TO BE THE ONES TO LEAVE.

IN MY OWN MISGUIDED WAY, I WAS TRYING TO CREATE SOME STABILITY FOR MY DOG.

124

BEIJA COULD EXPERIENCE JOY AND CLOSENESS AND AN INVIGORATING, MEANINGFUL DOG VERSION OF LIFE WITHOUT THE NEED FOR STRANGE HUMAN HANDS UPON HER COARSE FUR-COVERED BODY.

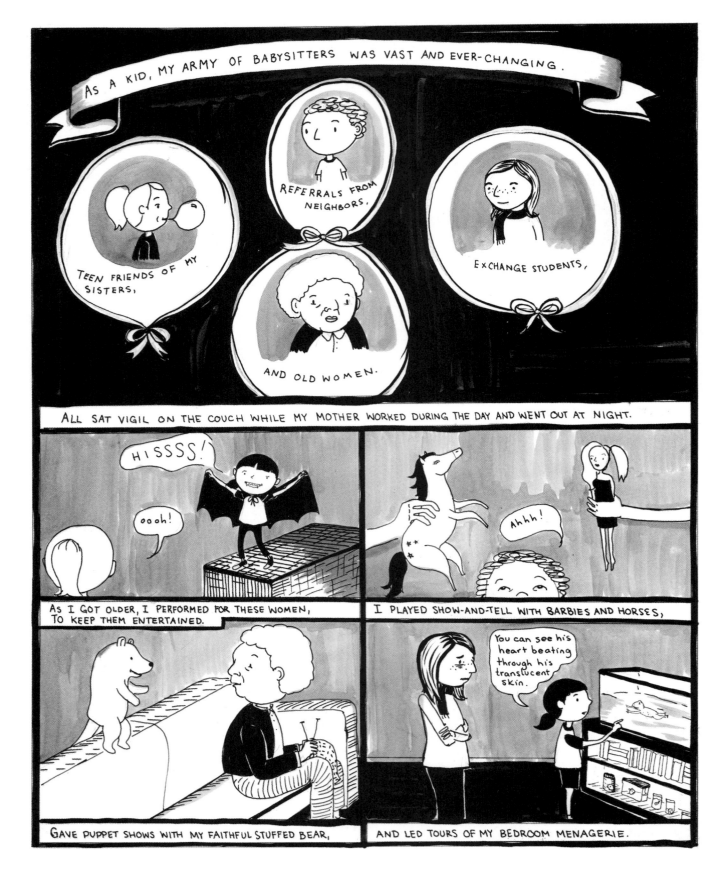

As a kid, my army of babysitters was vast and ever-changing.

Teen friends of my sisters,

Referrals from neighbors,

Exchange students,

And old women.

All sat vigil on the couch while my mother worked during the day and went out at night.

HISSSS!

ooh!

As I got older, I performed for these women, to keep them entertained.

Ahhh!

I played show-and-tell with barbies and horses,

Gave puppet shows with my faithful stuffed bear,

You can see his heart beating through his translucent skin.

And led tours of my bedroom menagerie.

126

4. Easy, Girl

a musical

Interlude

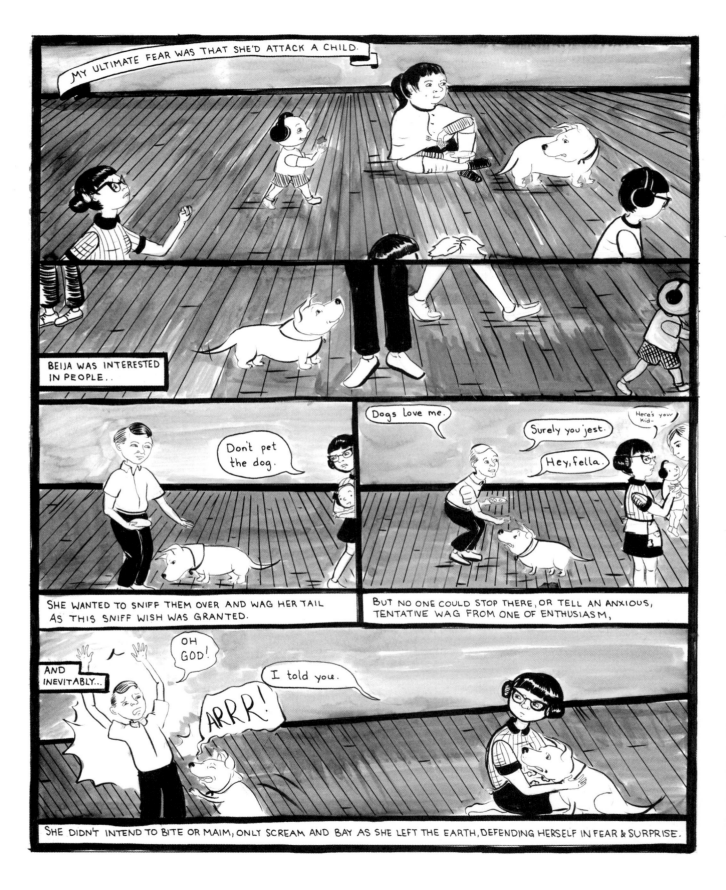

140

143

THE PEOPLE WHO GOT IT— WHO LISTENED AND ADJUSTED— WERE (EVENTUALLY) REWARDED WITH LIFELONG DOG FRIENDSHIP.

I almost cried when she first jumped in my lap.

It's like I really earned it.

You're in Beija's inner circle!

SHE RECOGNIZED AND CAME TO THEM, WAGGING AND SMILING.

THOSE WHO WERE ALWAYS SCARED AND ANXIOUS SET OFF HER ALARMS. IN SOME CASES, THEY NEVER OVERCAME IT.

Hey, ... Beija.

She can tell you don't like her.

It's best if you don't.

FROM LARGE TO SMALL, EVERYONE WANTED A PIECE OF HER.

AND THEY GOT IT.

SNAP!

BEIJA WAS NOT A FIGHTER.

SHE WAS FEARFUL AND SHE FRONTED, SHE EVEN TRIED TO DOMINATE OTHER DOGS FOR ABOUT THREE SECONDS,

arrrp!

BUT WHEN DOGS LEAPT UPON HER, SHE SCREAMED AND CRIED AND ROLLED ON HER BACK, GETTING BITTEN AND SLICED AND CHEWED.

Real scene of 2 dogs (one blind) tag-teaming her.

Why do they always go for the face?

She's a shar-pei! It's the extra skin!

She looks like someone who's had their face through a windshield.

Oh, Beija!

BASED ON THIS, SHE ACCRUED A FACE OF SCARS FROM FIGHTS.

155

SHE HAD SCARS ON TOP OF SCARS, THE MINOR DISFIGUREMENT BEING PREFERABLE TO THE TRAUMA OF A VETERINARIAN'S TOUCH.

Well, if you get stitches, it won't scar as bad,

but given how she's reacting, I'd say you don't need to.

and she already has a hamburger face.

You hear that?

You get to go!

BEIJA WAS BEAUTIFUL TO ME. I ACCEPTED HER AS SHE WAS, IMPERFECT AND MINE.

THESE WERE HER EXPERIENCES, CARVED OUT ON HER DEAR SHAR-PEI FACE.
I WOULDN'T HAVE CHANGED HER APPEARANCE, BUT I DID WORRY FOR HER SAFETY,
AND THE TRAUMA IT CAUSED MY GIRL EACH TIME SHE WAS ATTACKED.

IN A SEA OF BABYSITTERS (AND FEW HUMAN FRIENDS TO SPEAK OF)
I FOUND INSPIRATION, AND A KINDRED SPIRIT, IN A WOMAN NAMED IRENE.

C'mon, Ginger, up up.

Hack Hack

IRENE WAS A WITCH, AN ASTROLOGER MY MOM PUT STOCK IN BEFORE GOING CATHOLIC.

MY MOM WOULD LEAVE ME AT IRENE'S HOUSE FOR DAYS AT A TIME WHILE SHE TENDED TO HER OWN ROMANTIC AFFAIRS.

She loves American cheese.

I've never seen a dog with painted nails before.

IRENE

IRENE WAS A CHAIN-SMOKER WHO LIVED ALONE IN A TRAILER CROWDED WITH DOLL PARTS, NEWSPAPERS, AND A POODLE.

GINGER HAD A POT BELLY FROM ALL THE CHEESE SHE EARNED ON HER HIND LEGS.

HER NAILS WERE ALWAYS PAINTED. SHE WAS AN APRICOT. SHE LOOKED SUN-FADED AND OLD, LIKE THE DOLLS ON IRENE'S WINDOWSILLS.

HER FUR SMELLED LIKE RICH CIGARETTE SMOKE.

GINGER

ON TOP OF BEING AN ASTROLOGER, IRENE ALSO BUILT AND MENDED DOLLS. I WALKED THE WALLS OF THE TRAILER LIKE IT WAS A MUSEUM, MARVELING AT THE TREASURES, PIECES YOU COULD USE TO CREATE NEW, BEAUTIFUL FRIENDS.

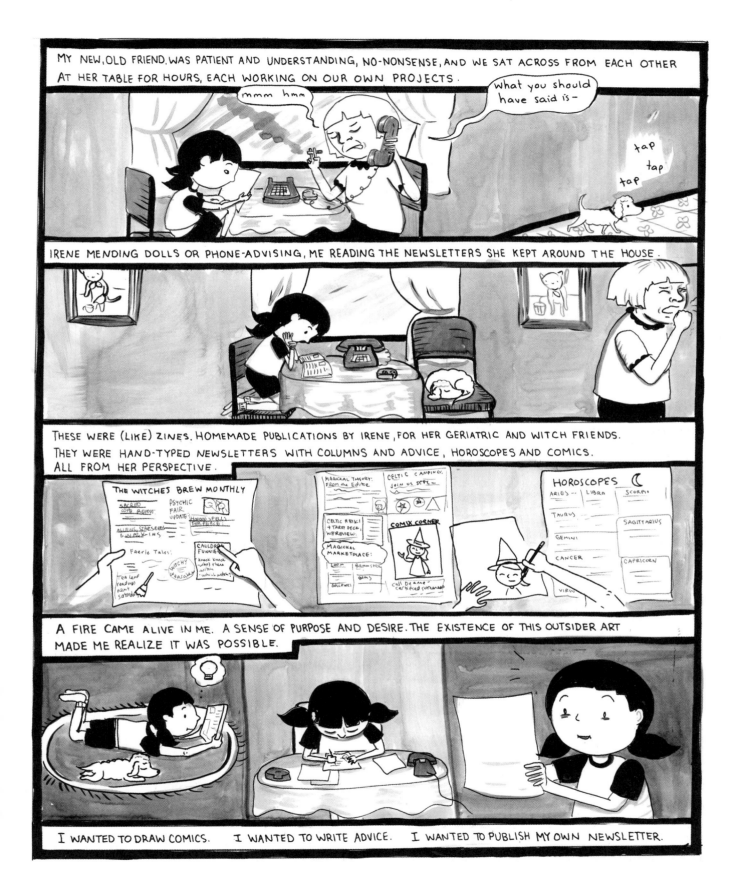

MY NEW, OLD FRIEND, WAS PATIENT AND UNDERSTANDING, NO-NONSENSE, AND WE SAT ACROSS FROM EACH OTHER AT HER TABLE FOR HOURS, EACH WORKING ON OUR OWN PROJECTS.

mmm hmm

what you should have said is—

tap tap tap

IRENE MENDING DOLLS OR PHONE-ADVISING, ME READING THE NEWSLETTERS SHE KEPT AROUND THE HOUSE.

THESE WERE (LIKE) ZINES. HOMEMADE PUBLICATIONS BY IRENE, FOR HER GERIATRIC AND WITCH FRIENDS. THEY WERE HAND-TYPED NEWSLETTERS WITH COLUMNS AND ADVICE, HOROSCOPES AND COMICS. ALL FROM HER PERSPECTIVE.

THE WITCHES BREW MONTHLY

HOROSCOPES

A FIRE CAME ALIVE IN ME. A SENSE OF PURPOSE AND DESIRE. THE EXISTENCE OF THIS OUTSIDER ART MADE ME REALIZE IT WAS POSSIBLE.

I WANTED TO DRAW COMICS.   I WANTED TO WRITE ADVICE.   I WANTED TO PUBLISH MY OWN NEWSLETTER.

OLD WOMEN'S HOUSES FEEL LIKE THE SAFEST PLACE ON EARTH. A SHRINE TO FUNCTIONAL FEMININITY. IRENE'S HOUSE WAS A PEACEFUL SANCTUARY. THE ONLY CHAOS CAME FROM HER OWN PILES OF TREASURES AND TASKS. SHE WAS TOUGH, AND SHE HAD IT UNDER CONTROL. I LOVED IT THERE.

I LOVED IT THERE, BUT BIOLOGY STRUCK, AND EVENTUALLY I WOULD START GETTING NERVOUS THAT MY MOM WOULDN'T RETURN.

IRENE'S AGE AND HEALTH INTERSECTED WITH MY YOUNG-PERSON ANXIETY AND FEAR OF BEING ABANDONED. I WOULD LISTEN TO HER BREATHING IN THE EARLY MORNING HOURS, COUNTING THE APNEATIC BREAKS AND THE IMPOSSIBLE COUGHING. IRENE'S SMOKER'S COUGH GOT SCARY. TOO DEEP AND WET AND REAL.

I WAS CONSTANTLY PREPARING TO CALL 911 IN THOSE HOURS AROUND DAWN, SO CONVINCED THE WORST WOULD HAPPEN.

5. Speak

MARTY KNEW I WAS BROKE AND DID NOT MAKE ME PAY LUCIFER'S VET BILL, DESPITE THE CULPABILITY OF BEIJA AND ME.

Hey, daddio

...and here's one I did of Alex from *A Clockwork Orange*.

These are great.

I EVEN TRIED TO TAKE ART CLASSES BASED ON MY ABILITY TO RE-CREATE A TURTLE BEATNIK.

A REPRESENTATIVE OF THE CORRESPONDENCE ART SCHOOL CAME TO MY HOUSE.

I'll be in touch!

too expensive

BUT THIS WAS NOT MY PATH EITHER.

MOMENTARILY DEFLATED, I STOPPED DRAWING FOR A WHILE. I SCUTTERED INTO A WORLD OF ZINES. I FAVORED FIRST-PERSON NARRATIVES, PUNK MUSIC, AND THE UNDERGROUND.

KING CAT
MUFFin bones #18
DIRTY-PLOTTE
assassin and the whiner 15

THROUGH ZINES I FOUND DIARY COMICS, AND SOMETHING CLICKED STRONGLY INTO PLACE.

YOU DIDN'T NEED SUPERHEROES OR GAGS. A PERSON COULD DRAW HER OWN LIFE.

SOMETHING ABOUT BEIJA AS AN ALLY (AND CONSTANT SOURCE OF DRAMA AND JOY) INSPIRED ME TO START DRAWING AGAIN. IT WAS LIKE HOW I'D PLAYED WITH MY PETS AS A KID. OUR OWN INTROVERTED WORLD, NOW TRANSFORMED INTO SOMETHING NEW I COULD SHARE AND USE AS A BRIDGE.

SHE WAS MY MUSE. A DISTINCT CHARACTER WHOM I COULD VOCALIZE AND BOUNCE OFF OF. AN EXTERNALIZATION OF SOMETHING I'D BEEN TRYING TO SAY.

I BEGAN SELF-PUBLISHING COMICS ABOUT MY SIDEKICK AND ME. I DREW OUR DAYS, CONSTRUCTED SMALL STORIES, AND PHOTOCOPIED THESE EXPERIENCES TIRELESSLY. I FELT COMPELLED TO SHARE HER.

THE ROOMMATES HAD JOKINGLY STARTED CALLING ME "MOMMY" OR "MOTHER" AFTER HEARING ME SAY IT TO THE DOG, BUT NOW THE BURDEN WAS TOO REAL.

I HADN'T ANTICIPATED THE LONELINESS OF COUNTRY LIFE. IT WAS A STRANGE PLACE TO BE NEWLY GAY, AND MY COWORKERS WERE SCARCE AFTER THEIR 12-HOUR SHIFTS CONCLUDED.

UNABLE TO REACH OUT TO AVERY (FOR THE TIME BEING), THESE RICH MEMORIES WERE SHARED BETWEEN JUST BEIJA AND I. WE HAD A CALM, INVISIBLE CONNECTION. A MARRIAGE.

MY FEELINGS OF NEGLECT AND DISAPPOINTMENT CALCIFIED INTO AN INDIGESTIBLE STONE OF UNHEARD RAGE THAT LAUNCHED OUTWARD.

AND INEVITABLY, IMMEDIATELY, A SENSE THAT I'D BETRAYED MY ONLY COMPANIONS WASHED OVER ME.

6. Get Down

I BUCKLED MYSELF TO EARTH WITH A TASK, PAINTING A MEMORIAL PORTRAIT OF TWO CATS I'D HEARD ABOUT.

BROTHERS WHO'D DIED IN QUICK SUCCESSION, VICTIMS OF STREET TRAFFIC.

THE CATS BELONGED TO A FRIEND OF A FRIEND. A GIRL NAMED KIT.

I HAD TRIED EXORCISING MY DISPLACED FEELINGS ABOUT THE FARM AND AVERY VIA WOUNDED SELF-PORTRAITS AND SAD COMICS, BUT I FOUND REAL SATISFACTION BY IMBUING ANIMAL IMAGES WITH EMOTIONS INSTEAD.

IT FELT LESS LIKE SELF-PITY AND MORE LIKE FULFILLING MY POST-FARM SANCTUARY WISH.

SHE WAS SMALL AND SWEET, AND SHE UNDERSTOOD THE RULES OF A TEMPERAMENTAL ANIMAL BETTER THAN ANYONE SHOULD.

KIT UNDERSTOOD THE RULES SO WELL BECAUSE SHE, HERSELF, WAS LIKE AN ANIMAL. DATING HER REMINDED ME OF THE TIME I TRIED TO RESCUE FERAL KITTENS FROM THE WOODPILE.

I SHOULD HAVE RUN, OR EVEN CONSIDERED THIS A FLAG WORTH NOTING, BUT AS IT STOOD, THIS FELT NORMAL AND NATURAL.

AS SOON AS MY FEET LANDED IN PORTLAND, SHEILA THE PET PSYCHIC STARTED CALLING ME.

SHE WANTED ME TO HONE MY ANIMAL COMMUNICATION SKILLS FOR THE GOOD OF FARM ANIMALS,

WHEN I PROTESTED THAT I COULDN'T AFFORD HER CLASSES, SHE ARRANGED FOR GERIATRIC VEGANS TO SPONSOR ME.

I REMEMBERED THE FEELING OF BEIJA SPEAKING THROUGH SHEILA. THAT I WAS THE FIRST PERSON TO HOLD HER. WHAT IF THAT WAS REAL? WHAT IF I COULD DO THAT FOR FARM ANIMALS?

To La Center I go.

WELCOME TO OLYMPIA

AND SO I DROVE. I DROVE TOWARD SEATTLE, AT 6 O'CLOCK IN THE MORNING, BECAUSE I WANTED TO TRY AND HONE THIS LITERAL VERSION OF "SPEAKING FOR." TO BE HELPFUL.

pinch

z z z

THAT'S ALL I'D EVER WANTED TO DO.

I'D ANTICIPATED A THREE-HOUR DRIVE, BUT AT 9 AM, THE WORKSHOP'S START TIME,

LA CENTER STILL HADN'T SHOWN UP.

gasp!

214

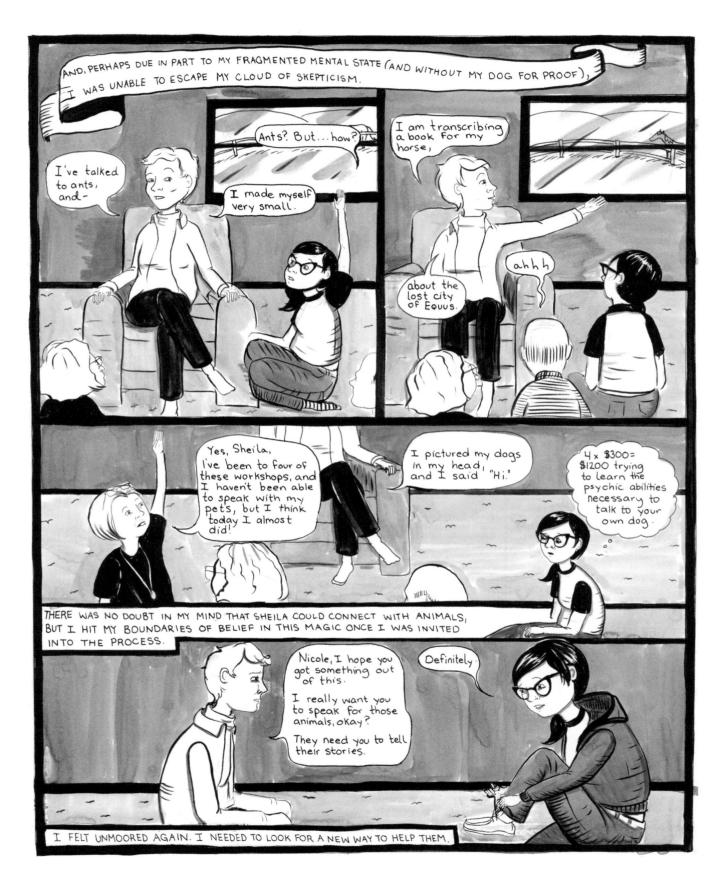

AND, PERHAPS DUE IN PART TO MY FRAGMENTED MENTAL STATE (AND WITHOUT MY DOG FOR PROOF), I WAS UNABLE TO ESCAPE MY CLOUD OF SKEPTICISM.

Ants? But...how?

I've talked to ants, and—

I made myself very small.

I am transcribing a book for my horse,

about the lost city of Equus.

ahhh

Yes, Sheila, I've been to four of these workshops, and I haven't been able to speak with my pets, but I think today I almost did!

I pictured my dogs in my head, and I said, "Hi."

4 × $300 = $1200 trying to learn the psychic abilities necessary to talk to your own dog.

THERE WAS NO DOUBT IN MY MIND THAT SHEILA COULD CONNECT WITH ANIMALS, BUT I HIT MY BOUNDARIES OF BELIEF IN THIS MAGIC ONCE I WAS INVITED INTO THE PROCESS.

Nicole, I hope you got something out of this.

I really want you to speak for those animals, okay?

They need you to tell their stories.

Definitely.

I FELT UNMOORED AGAIN. I NEEDED TO LOOK FOR A NEW WAY TO HELP THEM.

I GLITCHED OUT.

YOU DON'T START GOING TO THERAPY BECAUSE YOU'RE HAVING A GOOD TIME. IN FACT, THERE IS GENERALLY A "ROCK BOTTOM" TO CLIMB UP FROM WITH THE HELP OF A PROFESSIONAL ROPE.

KIT WAS MY ROCK BOTTOM.

I WAS 23.

THIS EVENT, THIS TREATMENT, REAWAKENED SOMETHING DEEP AND DARK. THE WIRES BOUND UP IN ME, THE ONES I THOUGHT WERE GONE OR INVISIBLE. ANGRY FRACTURES AND A CAPACITY FOR LEARNED VIOLENCE—THIS CONFIRMED THAT SOMEONE ELSE COULD SEE THEM.

THESE FRACTURES WERE REAL, AND MAYBE DESPITE OUR BEST EFFORTS, BEIJA AND I DID NOT DESERVE NORMAL TREATMENT.

KIT HAD FINELY TUNED ANTENNAE FOR SUSSING OUT WEAKNESS. SHE SPIT THESE SOFT SPOTS INTO MY FACE ON THE WAY OUT THE DOOR.

Just go then.

I DIDN'T THINK I COULD GO ANY LOWER.

I SUBSEQUENTLY DID.

You never loved me anyway.

You only love that crazy dog.

I BROKE UP WITH KIT.

ALL HER INITIAL SWEETNESS
THAT I'D STORED UP TO
JUSTIFY STAYING
RUSTED AND MELDED
WITH THE HARD COILED
WIRES LEFT IN MY CHEST.
THEY DUG IN, HISSING
THAT I WAS A FOOL
FOR NOT HEEDING
SIGNALS ALONG
THE WAY.

MY DEEPEST ANIMAL BRAIN
WANTED TO STAY.

I DIDN'T WANT TO KILL MYSELF BECAUSE I HAD A BAD GIRLFRIEND WHO KICKED MY DOG. I WANTED TO KILL MYSELF BECAUSE SHE SEEMED TO CONFIRM SOMETHING I WAS DEEPLY AFRAID OF.

THAT I WASN'T WORTH IT.

I'm sorry I'm sorry I'm sorry I'm sorry.

BEING CHOSEN. BEING LOVED LIKE THAT. THE SECRET FEELING THAT THE SUN SHINING ON MY FACE JUST DIDN'T KNOW ME WELL ENOUGH. IF IT SAW ME FOR ME, UNWORTHY AND FERAL, IT WOULD TURN AWAY. THE SUN ITSELF.

SCREEE!

What are you gonna do, kill me?

screee!

HONNNK!

THESE DARK FEELINGS CAME UP IN ME AND CROWDED OUT THE (LARGELY SELF-MANUFACTURED) LIGHT.

THEY WERE AMPLIFIED BY THE FACT THAT I'D ALLOWED MY CHARGE, MY BEIJA, TO FOLLOW ME INTO A DANGEROUS SITUATION.

I HADN'T JUST BEEN SELF-DESTRUCTIVE, I'D LED HER THERE.

I IMAGINED I'D DESTROYED HER HARD-WON TRUST IN ME.

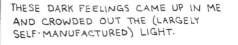

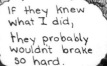

If they knew what I did, they probably wouldn't brake so hard.

I HAD THIS IMPULSE

THIS "FUCK IT, I'M FINISHED"
THOUGHT,

EVERY TIME I CROSSED THE BRIDGE.
MY HANDLEBARS WILLED THEMSELVES
TOWARD THE WATER. MY IMAGE OF
HITTING ITS SURFACE FELT
WHOLLY SATISFYING, LIKE CLOSURE
OF THIS BAD TIME.

I WANT TO TELL YOU THAT BEIJA SAVED ME. THAT IT WAS ONLY FOR HER THAT I WENT ON. BUT TRUTHFULLY, I IMAGINED HER HAVING A LONG QUIET LIFE WITH AVERY. A SAD FLAG OF WHERE I'D BEEN.

AS IT WAS, IT WAS MY INTERNAL BABYSITTER, THE ORGAN I'D GROWN IN CHILDHOOD TO TAKE CARE OF MYSELF WHEN NO ONE ELSE WOULD, THAT PROPELLED ME FORWARD. I PEDALED OFF THE BRIDGE, OUT OF TRAFFIC, AND BEIJA WAS THERE WHEN I GOT HOME.

BARK! BARK!

FORGIVING AND EARNEST, HEARTBREAKINGLY FAITHFUL, BEIJA LOVED ME EVEN WHEN I LAPSED IN LOVING MYSELF.

NEITHER OF US HAD EVER BEEN CHOSEN, BUT WE CHOSE EACH OTHER.

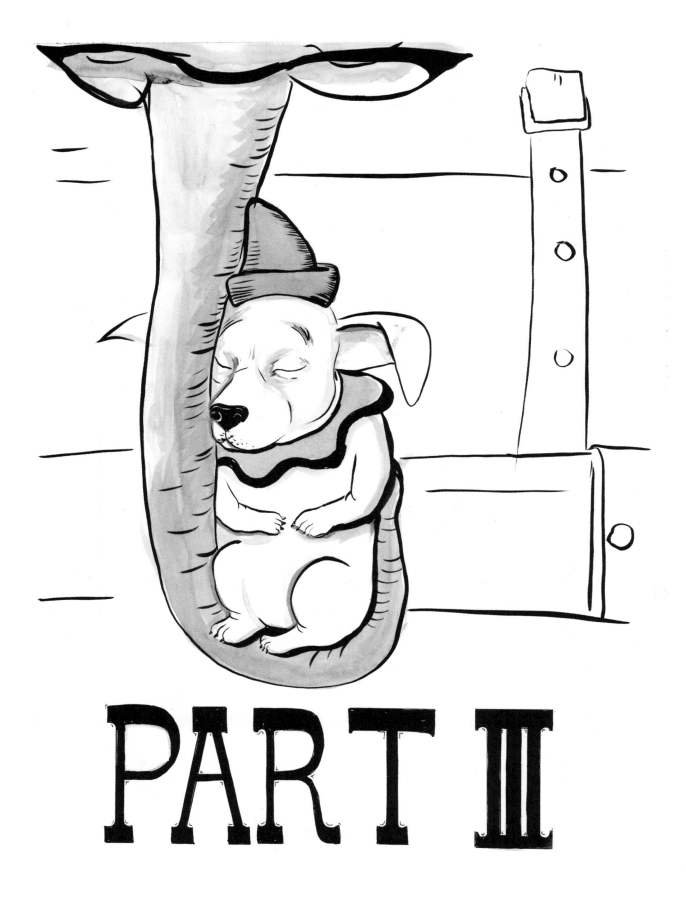

PART III

7. Heel

239

240

I HAD TRIED TO COMMUNICATE TO BEIJA ON HUMAN TERMS OF REFLECTION AND EMOTION. NOW I WAS READY TO SPEAK WITH HER ON CANINE TERMS.

I COULD BE THE LEADER OF THE WOLF PACK I'D DREAMT OF AS A CHILD.

TO LIVE IN THE MOMENT AND TRANSMIT CONFIDENCE, I HAD TO STOP PROTECTING US FROM THE CHAOTIC PAST,

AND ACCEPT THAT WITHOUT THAT TENSION, THOSE GUARDS, EVERYTHING COULD STILL BE OKAY.

IT HAD TO BE AN ACTIVE PRACTICE. A ZEN VERSION OF MY OLD HYPERVIGILANCE.

THERE WAS SOMETHING ELSE, TOO, THAT BOTHERED ME ABOUT SUCH A DENSITY OF COHABITANTS. I NEEDED TO LIMIT, OR FEEL SOME CONTROL OVER, THE VIEWERS IN MY LIFE.

We made a book!

I'D BEEN PUBLISHING AUTOBIOGRAPHICAL COMICS FOR YEARS ABOUT BEIJA AND ME, AND WE STARTED TO GET NOTICED.

I hate men!

She's the best!

You idiots!

I HAD DRAWN ABOUT US, AND IN TURN HAD BEEN DRAWN ABOUT. THE COMIC VERSIONS OF "NICOLE" AND "BEIJA" WERE EXAGGERATED, AND NASTIER THAN I EVER FELT. WHEN WE WERE RECOGNIZED, THIS IS WHAT PEOPLE SAW.

So cute!

Don't pet that dog, she's mean. I read about her in a comic book.

Thanks for letting me know—I almost pet her!

Well, she's actually just shy.

Oh, I thought you were going to be a lot meaner.

But... we've never met...

From the comics.

WHEN THIS HAPPENED TO MY DOG IN PUBLIC, I WAS HER DEFENDER. WHEN IT HAPPENED TO ME, I JUST WANTED TO HIDE.

255

257

267

8. Good Dog

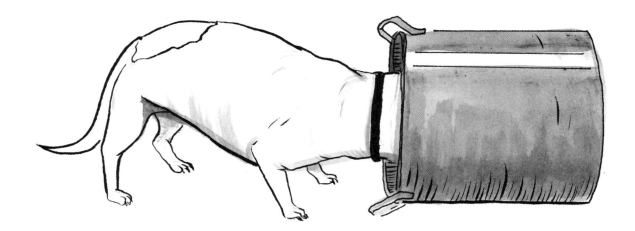

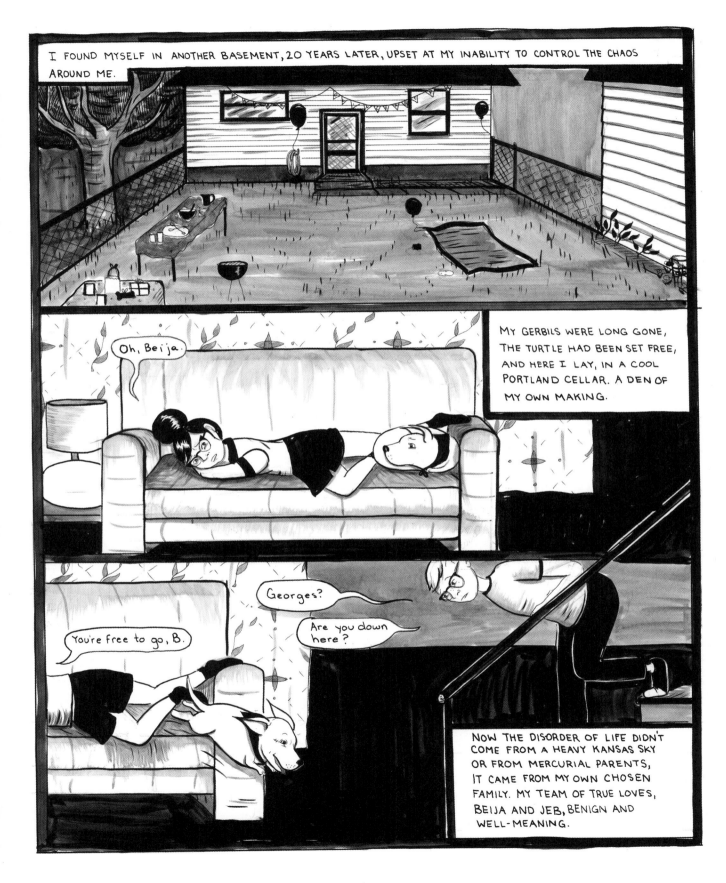

MY SPRY, HEALTHY, FIFTEEN-YEAR-OLD BEST FRIEND HAD A BUMP,

DREAD WASHED OVER ME AT THE SIGHT.

"THE TYPE OF MEMORY THAT TURNS YOUR BONES TO GLASS."

IN SERVICE TO HER STAYING, WE VISITED A SURGEON.

1. DO NOTHING
EXCISIONAL BIOPSY
RADIATION

To even try to save her life will cost thousands of dollars.

THE DIAGNOSIS WAS REAL, AND SURGERY WAS ON THE TABLE.
EXCISION OF HER TUMOR.

I HAD NOTHING.
NO SAVINGS, NO CREDIT,
NO WAY TO HELP MY DOG.

I QUESTIONED MY ENTIRE PROFESSIONAL LIFE.

Beija, I'm so sorry.

((Heave))

I've spent all this time working at non-profits and on art... hic ... and I can't... snort ... afford.... hic to save your life.

I'm such a fucking idiot.
I spent so much time honoring other people's pets that...

Sob

I WAS CRUSHED. I'D CRUSHED MYSELF. HER GOING DOWN WITHOUT A FIGHT AFTER THIS HARD-WON LIFE MADE ME SICK TO MY STOMACH.

Oh my God, what am I going to do?

I'm sorry, Beija. I'm sorry.

You deserve the best.

I would do anything.

A WORLD OF OLD ROOMMATES, BANDMATES, FRIENDS, AND FANS. READERS OF MY DOG AND MY DRAWINGS. I WROTE TO THEM. I FELT LIKE I WAS TELLING EVERYONE PERSONALLY- THIS IS IT. OUR FRIEND IS DYING. OUR GIRL IS GOING DOWN.

REGARDING MY EXTERNAL HEART, BEIJA GEORGES

Hello friends.
Beija Georges was diagnosed with a cancerous tumor today.
She has a soft tissue sarcoma.

I had to drug her for the occasion. She usually dons a muzzle at the vet's office, from which she hyperventilates and yelps and struggles.
It's traumatic for everyone, so for the first time in 15 years I planned ahead. I put a pill into her favorite food (the tomato) and as I was feeding her I had a moment of guilt for tricking my best friend.
I announced out loud, "I put a 'downer in this 'tomato", as I was handing it to her, and she gingerly accepted it in her velvety shar-pei lips anyway.

As I was waiting for it to kick in, she was prancing around the house, approaching me several times to give me a dog kiss.
It was nice and a little heartbreaking, since I knew she was going in for something that was likely cancer.
But the prancing and the dog kisses seemed like Beija showing (if not telling) me that she enjoys living. She enjoys this life that she has. She wags her tail, she eats tomatoes, chews kale stalks, hoards dog bones, and skids across the floor chasing her tennis ball.

ANYWAY, by the time we were seen in the vet's office, Beija was practically asleep, involved in probably the worst stoner daze of all time, in which she got poked, prodded, and biopsied.

Her very kind veterinarian found a heart murmur, rotten teeth, and, of course, the cancer.

The cancer is the #1 thing on my mind.

This particular kind of tumor is not known for spreading, and is easy to remove. The placement of it makes things precarious (its near her dear spine), but the vet (thus far) seemed confident that this was something that, if taken care of, could keep cancer out of the picture either forever, or for a good long while.

So far, my vet's estimates are that the cancer procedure will cost approximately $1500. If she needs an MRI to suss out the tumor's proximity to her spine & nerves it could be an additional $1500-$2000.
I do not have an estimate from the heart specialist yet.

Beija's upcoming bills already outpace my savings account, so I humbly present a donation button and ask you, my community of dog lovers (and maybe specifically Beija lovers), to consider helping us out in this time of need.

If you are an animal appreciator, a "crotchety-dog-depicted-in comics" lover, or have ever met or felt fondness toward Beija or myself, please consider donating even the smallest scrap towards her veterinary fund. Even if it's $5.

Please wish us safe voyage on this frightening new journey.

Thank you for considering it, from the bottom of my heart.
Sincerely, Nicole J. Georges

WITH THEIR DONATIONS, EVERYTHING FELT LIKE IT WAS GOING TO BE OKAY. WE COULD AFFORD TO FIGHT.

284

WE ADDED A CARDIOLOGIST TO THE ROTATION IN PREPARATION FOR SURGERY, AND STARTED SEEING A HOLISTIC VET FOR AN ALTERNATIVE APPROACH. THEIR KINDNESS WAS OVERWHELMING. I STOPPED ROLLING TAPE AS THEY SPOKE, WASHED OVER IN DREAD AS I WAS, AND BROUGHT MY FRIEND MARTY TO TAKE NOTES AND CONFIRM WHAT WAS SAID.

I BROUGHT BEIJA HOME ON A RAINY NIGHT. JEB WAS OUT OF TOWN, AND I HAD TWO FRIENDS STAYING OVER TO KEEP THE HOUSE WARM.

Do you need help?

No, no, stay!

It's great.

Are you sure we should stay?

I MANIACALLY TRIED TO HOST THEM AS I PUT THE PIECES OF MY DOG BACK TOGETHER, PRETENDING TO BE HUMAN INSTEAD OF THE WOUNDED ANIMAL I'D BECOME.

I LOVE YOU

Here. You are protected with love.

Okay, Haji Monchi

You stay. Sleep tight.

SHE RECUPERATED IN HER KENNEL, AND I THOUGHT EVERYTHING WOULD BE OKAY. AND IT WAS.

Stew!

BEIJA HAD A 10-INCH SCAR WHERE SHE'D BEEN SEWN UP, WITH A RECTANGLE OF MISSING HAIR THAT STARTED TO SLOWLY GROW BACK, A WHITE FUZZY UNDERCOAT LIKE SPRINGTIME.

SHE SHOVED HER WAY AROUND WITH THE CONE, AND RAN WAGGING FOR STEW EACH MORNING.

grrrr

grrr

I HAD A BOOK COMING OUT SOON, MY FIRST GRAPHIC NOVEL, AND WE POSED FOR PHOTOS TOGETHER. I NARRATED OUR STORY FOR REPORTERS.

JEB MUST HAVE BEEN THERE. SHE SAYS SHE FED BEIJA HER LAST TOMATO, BUT I DON'T REMEMBER ANYTHING.
ALL I CAN SEE IS THAT MOMENT.
HERE'S HOW MEMORY WORKS—IN THAT MOMENT, I'M ALONE. JUST ME, THE VET, A TECH, MY GIRL.

THEY COULDN'T FIND A VEIN,
HAD TO TIE HER SMALL ARM
OFF LIKE A JUNKIE,
UGLY AND UNDIGNIFIED.

A SHUDDER RAN THROUGH ME
AS I HELD BEIJA STILL
TO PUT HER DOWN.

She's gone.

302

303

R.I.P.
My "Haji Monchi"
grrr
Dont growl at me, Beija,
If I really wanted a bone, I could just go buy my own.
Give me a break.

THE WEEK AFTER BEIJA DIED, I HAD TO LEAVE HOME FOR A BOOK TOUR. I HAD TO BE MY OWN BRUTAL STAGE MOM. I COULDN'T TALK ABOUT IT. I JUST HAD TO STAY IN MOTION, READING, DRAWING, DRIVING.

I love the pictures of your dog online with her head in the stew pot.

Keep it up!

Oh!

I'll... try.

TO ME, DRAWING SOMEONE IS LIKE CASTING A PROTECTION SPELL OVER THEM, AN ATTEMPT TO HONOR AND UNDERSTAND AND KEEP THEM SAFE. SO THAT'S WHAT I DID.

for you

I DREW SO MANY DOGS, WANDS TO THE SKY, HOLDING FLOWERS TO HONOR AND PROTECT BEIJA IN HER PASSING. ON HER JOURNEY.

I left home, but you are with me.

ALL ACROSS THE WORLD, HIDING ON BOOKSHELVES AND IN BACKPACKS, ALL HOLDING A LOVE AND PROTECTION SPELL. A PRAYER FOR MY GIRL.

Epilogue

HUMAN WORDS FAILED ME, BUT THOSE WHO KNEW, REALLY KNEW.
I COULD FEEL THE WEIGHT OF THEIR OWN UNDERSTANDING.

THANK YOU

Fetch would not exist if not for the following humans:
Holly Bemiss, Nicole Angeloro, Christopher Moisan & Asher Craw,
Beth Fuller, Katrina Kruse & Stephanie Kim,
Rose City Blue Print, Michael Bland,
Productivity Coach Alec Longstreth,
Eagle-eyed Chelsey Johnson & Sarah Dougher,
Erasers Morgan Grundstein Helvey & Magda Gianola.

This book was made possible in part by a project grant by
The Regional Arts & Culture Council
& by the spaces, support, students & faculty of
The Center for Cartoon Studies,
The College of William & Mary
& California College of the Arts.

Thank you Carson Ellis & Colin Meloy for the farmspiration,
& to Team Dresch for the use of their song "Freewheel."
Thank you everyone at Cambourakis.

Thank you to Bill Callahan for writing the perfect line, "The type of memory that turns your bones to glass."

Thank you Aaron Renier, Jon Chad, Liz Prince, Greg Means, Brandie Taylor, Mathew New,
Alison Bechdel, Eileen Myles, Michelle Tea, Beth Pickens & Mary Beth Ditto.

The idea for this book came from bouncing the premise off of Chris Ware.

Thank you Tim, Aubree, Katy, Torrence, Natalie, Mary R., Diane, my sisters, Dawn,
Farm Sanctuary & every person who loved Beija in spite of her defenses.

Shout out to my life partner, Ponyo Georges.

Thank you Phoebe Gloeckner & Lynda Barry for being kind & making work that changed my life.

In loving memory of Genevieve Castree.